THE LITTLE BOOK OF
FOLKLORE

KITTY GREENBROWN

summersdale

THE LITTLE BOOK OF FOLKLORE

Copyright © Octopus Publishing Group Limited, 2024

Kitty Greenbrown has asserted their right to be identified as the author of this work in accordance with sections 77 and 78 of the Copyright, Designs and Patents Act 1988.

An Hachette UK Company
www.hachette.co.uk

Summersdale Publishers
Part of Octopus Publishing Group Limited
Carmelite House
50 Victoria Embankment
LONDON
EC4Y 0DZ
UK

www.summersdale.com

Printed and bound in Poland

ISBN: 978-1-83799-321-5

Substantial discounts on bulk quantities of Summersdale books are available to corporations, professional associations and other organizations. For details contact general enquiries: telephone: +44 (0) 1243 771107 or email: enquiries@summersdale.com.

✦ CONTENTS ✦

4 INTRODUCTION

6 CHAPTER ONE: The Beginnings of the British Isles

30 CHAPTER TWO: The Natural World

58 CHAPTER THREE: Creatures and Monsters

92 CHAPTER FOUR: Legendary Heroes

122 FAREWELL

124 FURTHER READING

✦ INTRODUCTION ✦

British folklore takes us back to a time of monsters and magic, when giants walked and hills offered doors to other realms. Tales spun around the hearth, during feasts and over cribs were brought to life by each teller, before being lovingly passed down from generation to generation so new eyes could shine with wonder as they drank in the meaning.

These colourful threads of shared belief have enabled us to explore both the world around us and within us for thousands of years, helping us triumph over evil, explore our darkest desires and wrestle with love, death and loss, all from the safety of our firesides.

Folklore has also allowed us to weave an intricate tapestry of customs that we still use today to celebrate and honour life events and rejoice in the cycle of the seasons.

While fairy tales are often set in imagined worlds and myths deal with deities, folklore is deeply rooted in the landscape. It's as rich and earthy as the soil beneath our feet, and just as full of life.

We hope you enjoy this whistle-stop tour of Britain's hill forts, heroes and hellhounds. While it isn't exhaustive, it is incredibly good fun.

CHAPTER ONE:

THE BEGINNINGS OF THE BRITISH ISLES

When it comes to explaining how the British Isles were formed, folklore does it in style. It offers wild and colourful tales of how the land was shaped and peopled, from the story of the wizard Merlin conjuring enormous stones from Ireland to form Stonehenge, to the tale of the goddess the Cailleach creating Ben Nevis with blows of her magical hammer.

It's difficult to know whether these creation myths were ever intended to be truly believed. They may just have been designed to explain the inexplicable or to teach moral lessons, like how trickery and greed don't always pay off while bravery will always win the day.

Either way, they take us on a gloriously bumpy ride through the history of Britain and how it came to be.

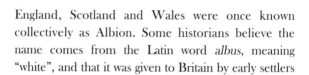

✦ THE KINGDOM OF ALBION ✦

England, Scotland and Wales were once known collectively as Albion. Some historians believe the name comes from the Latin word *albus*, meaning "white", and that it was given to Britain by early settlers when they first caught sight of the white cliffs of Dover.

Folklore, however, offers a more colourful explanation: one which involves wayward princesses, murder and giants.

THE LEGEND OF PRINCESS ALBINA

According to Geoffrey of Monmouth's *History of the Kings of Britain*, written in the late 1130s, the kingdom of Albion takes its name from a mythical princess called Albina. Albina, it is said, was sent to Britain as an exile with her 32 wayward sisters somewhere back in the mists of time.

The 33 princesses were supposedly cast out of their homeland by their father, the Roman Emperor Diocletian, for murdering their husbands, who they felt were unworthy of them. When they arrived in Albion, they found a green and pleasant land populated by animals and plants of all kinds but no other human beings.

Arriving as widows in an unpopulated land, the young women were forced to take the demon spirits of Albion's hills, rivers and caves as their lovers.

The legend goes that as a result of these wild unions, the sisters gave birth to a race of violent and unruly giants who ruled over Albion until Brutus of Troy arrived. With the help of his army and trusted general Corineus, Brutus then wiped out the giants.

According to folklore, the last remaining giant was a fearsome fellow called Gogmagog, who stood 12 cubits high and ruled over the south-west of England.

Eventually, Gogmagog was also overpowered by Corineus, who defeated him in battle, picked him up and then heaved him off Plymouth Hoe. According to Geoffrey of Monmouth, Corineus then gave his name to Cornwall, while Brutus founded London.

✦ GOG AND MAGOG ✦

Carved statues of Gogmagog and Corineus stand in the Guildhall in London today and have done so since 1554.

Over time, the Guildhall giants have become known as Gog and Magog, leading some people to associate them with another version of the myth where two giants, rather than one, were defeated in the final battle for control of windswept Albion.

In this variant of the story, Brutus and Corineus jointly tackled the last two survivors of the violent race of giants descended from Albina and her sisters: two terrible fiends known as Gog and Magog.

Once they had been defeated, the story then tells how Brutus dragged the two enormous prisoners back to London and chained the warrior giants to the gates of Brutus' palace on the site of the modern-day Guildhall. The two were then kept there to act as guardians.

By whichever route Gog and Magog arrived at their guarding post, it is well known that by the time Henry V was on the throne, the carved giants were firmly positioned at the gates of the Guildhall.

Whether you prefer the version of the story with one giant or two, the Guildhall statues offer a fascinating link back to Albina and the folk-tale origins of the British Isles.

Every year, on the second Sunday of November, effigies of Gog and Magog are carried through the City of London as part of the traditional procession in the Lord Mayor's Show.

The tall figures seen on the day of the show are just the latest in a long line of pagan effigies that go back at least a thousand years.

✦ BRUTUS AND BRITAIN ✦

How did Brutus of Troy come to be in Albion in the first place? What happened after he'd dispatched the last of the native giants?

The story of Brutus appears first in the ninth-century *Historia Brittonum*, written by the chronicler Nennius, and later in Geoffrey of Monmouth's *History of the Kings of Britain*. According to both accounts, Brutus was exiled from Troy for accidentally killing his father with an arrow while out hunting.

Geoffrey of Monmouth then explains how Brutus set sail in a ship loaded with provisions and landed in Greece. The story describes how Brutus freed some fellow Trojans who were enslaved there, overthrew the king of Greece and married his daughter Ignoge, before taking to the seas again.

After a short war with the Gauls, Brutus and his army landed in Totnes in Devon and claimed Albion as their own. Brutus declared that the goddess Diana had shown him this fertile land in a dream and told him that he was destined to settle there and rule.

Once they'd settled in Albion, Brutus and his generals saw off the native giants and divided the kingdom between themselves, changing its name to Britain and calling their subjects "Britons" after their great leader.

According to Geoffrey of Monmouth, they subsequently created a city called "New Troy", or "Trinovantum", on the banks of the Thames. We now know this city as London.

In Geoffrey's account, Brutus ruled over Britain for 24 years and had three sons by Ignoge – Locrinus, Albanactus and Kamber.

When Brutus died, the kingdom was divided between his sons, with the exception of Cornwall, which was ruled by the giant-killing Corineus. Locrinus became ruler of Loegria, which is modern-day England (minus Cornwall). Albanactus ruled Albania or Albany, which is today's Scotland, and Kamber ruled over Cambria, the area now known as Wales.

✦ BRITAIN'S RELATIONS ✦ WITH IRELAND

On a clear day, you can make out the snowy peaks of Yr Wyddfa (Mount Snowdon) in Wales from across the Irish Sea. Given how close Wales and Ireland are physically, it's no surprise there are many folk tales about how their relationship was formed.

THE TALE OF BRANWEN

This story touches on the ancient relations between the Irish and the British, explaining how Ireland came to be divided into provinces. The tale of Branwen comes from a famous Welsh collection called *The Mabinogion*, written in the twelfth and thirteenth centuries. However, the stories are believed to be much older.

According to *The Mabinogion*, Britain was once ruled by a Welsh king, Bendigeidfran, which means "blessed raven". He was also known as Brân for short. Brân was a giant who lived in a castle on Harlech Rock with his sister Branwen, brother Manawydan and half-brother Efnisien, who was known for his bad temper and impulsive behaviour.

One day, King Brân and his family saw ships approaching from Ireland. The fleet had their shields raised in peace and was led by Matholwch, king of Ireland. He had come to ask Brân for his sister's hand in marriage.

Brân agreed to the match, believing it would bring lasting peace between the two nations, and a lavish wedding took place. Yet Efnisien wasn't happy, as he felt he hadn't been properly consulted about the marriage. So he raised his sword and attacked Matholwch's horses, which were tethered outside.

When Matholwch discovered his injured horses, he was greatly offended and made ready to sail immediately for Ireland with his new bride.

To make peace, Brân gave Matholwch new horses to replace the injured ones, a thick silver ingot, a gold plate and a magic cauldron to heal the sick and bring the dead back to life.

When Queen Branwen arrived in Ireland, her beauty was much admired, and she was given exquisite gifts of jewellery. After a year, she gave birth to a baby son, Gwern, and everyone rejoiced.

However, trouble was brewing. Soon after Gwern's birth, the Irish nobles heard about Efnisien's attack on Matholwch's horses. They demanded that Matholwch punish Branwen in retaliation.

Matholwch gave in to the demands of his court and banished Branwen to work in the castle's kitchens, where she was beaten and forced to work long hours. He also forbade travel between Ireland and Wales to make sure that no word of his vengeance got back to King Brân.

Branwen had a miserable time in the kitchens. She was friendless, except for a young starling that had flown through the kitchen window one day. She fed and tamed her new companion and told the starling stories of her brave brother, the giant king back in Wales. She showed the starling the way to his castle across the water.

Once Branwen believed the starling was strong enough, she gave it a letter and told it to fly straight and true to her brother Brân. In the letter she told her brother of her imprisonment and betrayal by Matholwch and the Irish.

When Brân received the letter, he was furious. Fearing for his sister's life and the honour of his people, he gathered a mighty army and set sail across the Irish Sea. Brân himself had no need of a boat; with his enormous height, he simply waded across the water between Wales and Ireland.

Matholwch was afraid of Brân and when he heard reports of his army crossing the sea, he fled across the River Shannon and destroyed the only existing bridge.

Crossing the river was no problem for Brân. He simply lay down so his men could cross on his back, uttering the words: "He that would lead, let him be a bridge." This phrase is still a well-known Welsh proverb.

When Matholwch saw that the Welsh had crossed the Shannon, he panicked and offered Brân a truce. He promised to put his son, Gwern, on the Irish throne in his stead and build a giant house for Brân if he would end the conflict.

Brân agreed, but when the giant house was finished, it transpired that 100 Irish soldiers had been secretly hidden in flour bags inside the house. Efnisien discovered the plot and, suspecting treachery, he crushed each of the men alive in their sacks.

That evening, things took an even uglier turn. Efnisien was enraged by the Irish betrayal and lost his temper during the peace talks between the two nations. Working himself into a frenzy, he ended his rampage by throwing his own nephew, Gwern, the king of Ireland, into the fire!

Branwen made to jump into the fire to rescue Gwern, but Brân held her back and the young king was swallowed up by the flames. It seemed all hope of peace had been lost, and bitter fighting broke out between the Irish and the Welsh.

With the magic cauldron Brân had given to Matholwch in their possession, the Irish found they could revive any soldier that fell in battle, which gave them a huge advantage over the Welsh. Efnisien saw this and realized he must act if they were to have any hope of victory.

Efnisien quickly hatched a plan which involved disguising himself as a dead Irish soldier so that he would be thrown into the cauldron. Once inside the enchanted pot, he used all his great strength to break the cauldron into four pieces from the inside, destroying it, and ending his own life in the process.

Without the cauldron, the two armies were evenly matched and the bloodshed was intense. Eventually, the Irish were defeated, but only seven Welsh soldiers remained alive, plus Brân and Branwen. With heavy hearts, the nine survivors set sail for Wales.

On the journey home, King Brân realized he'd been struck in the leg by a poisoned arrow during the final battle and he fell ill. He died before reaching home, but not before he had stated that upon his death his head was to be taken to London and buried at White Hill, looking south to prevent another invasion of Britain by sea.

White Hill is thought to be modern-day Tower Hill, the site of the Tower of London. It's been suggested that the tradition of keeping ravens at the Tower of London links back to King Brân, whose name means "blessed raven".

Branwen, meanwhile, died of a broken heart soon after returning to Wales. She was overcome by grief for the loved ones she'd lost. She was buried on the island of Anglesey.

Back in Ireland, the entire population had been wiped out by the conflict with the Welsh, all except for five expectant mothers who had hidden themselves inside a cave.

According to legend, these five mothers all gave birth to sons, who then each took one of the other' mothers as wives to bear them children. This way Ireland was slowly repopulated, and the land was divided into five districts, each ruled over by one of the sons.

The five kingdoms were called Connacht, Leinster, Munster, Ulster and Meath.

Connacht, famed for its learning, lay in the west. Leinster, known for hospitality, was positioned in the east. Munster, meanwhile, located in the south, was recognized for music and the arts. The northern kingdom of Ulster was known for its fearsome warriors.

The fifth kingdom of Meath was called the kingdom of the kings and the seat of the high king of Ireland was located there, at Tara Hill.

✦ HOW SCOTLAND WAS MADE ✦

Scotland has its own origin story, one which involves a powerful crone goddess known as the Cailleach, Dark Beira or Beira, Queen of Winter.

Beira is said to have created Scotland with her bare hands, dropping rocks into the vast North Sea from her skirts to create Scotland's many islands. She shaped Scotland's mountains with her magic hammer and gathered peat, which she carried in a creel on her back to lay out the moors and lowlands.

Scotland's rivers and lochs were formed from her mountain drinking wells. One story tells of how Loch Ness was created when one of Beira's maids, Nessa, forgot to put the lid back on a well one night and the water began flowing in great torrents down the hillside.

Beira was so angry with Nessa that she turned her into a river and the great Loch Ness was formed in the valley below.

Another tale tells of how Beira was out wading through the waters in the Firth of Clyde one day when a fishing boat sailed between her legs, brushing her thigh. Beira dropped the boulder she was carrying in surprise, and the small island of Ailsa Craig was formed.

As well as being the creation goddess and mother to all other gods and goddesses, Beira is also believed to be the Queen of Winter. She is often depicted with a blue face, white frost-covered hair and a single, piercing eye in the middle of her head.

She is said to have the power to call up storms and freeze the ground with her staff, keeping winter going for as long as she can. She was thought to rule from Samhain (around 1 November) to Beltane (around 1 May), when her counterpart Brid, Brigit or Bride, goddess of spring, took over.

Some stories tell of how, each Samhain, Beira would wash her giant plaid in the famous whirlpool of Corryvreckan, just off the coast of Jura in the Inner Hebrides. She would then spread her clean white plaid across the whole of Scotland and a blanket of snow would form.

THE WELL OF YOUTH

After the winter solstice, as the days lengthen and darkness begins to lose its grip on Scotland, Beira is said to travel to the Green Isle off the west coast to drink from the Well of Youth. Drinking its magic waters prolongs Beira's life, transforming her into a beautiful young goddess once more, with fair hair and rosy cheeks.

She walks the glens between Imbolc (around 1 February) and Samhain, dressed in a robe of green, herding deer and tending to her goats and cattle on the mountains.

As spring turns to summer, Beira enters womanhood. When autumn comes, she begins to age, before eventually taking on her crone form as the terrible Queen of Winter at Samhain.

✦ ANGUS AND BRID ✦

In many Cailleach stories, Beira has a husband called the Bodach and several giant sons. In these stories, her fairest son, Angus, King of Summer, caused a terrible rift with his mother by falling in love with Brid, goddess of spring.

In the legend of Angus and Brid, Angus dreamed of Brid and fell in love with her. He went to consult the king of the Green Isle to find her. Hearing of this, Beira imprisoned Brid inside Ben Nevis to prevent the two from meeting; she feared their union would bring about her end.

Angus learned where Brid was hidden from the king and, on the eve of Imbolc, he freed her. The two ran away with Beira in pursuit. A great battle for control of the land followed and Beira was forced to turn herself to stone to escape Angus.

In some versions of the story, Beira remains a stone until Samhain, when she once more captures Brid and imprisons her in Ben Nevis.

In other tellings, Angus and Brid flee from Beira to the Green Isle, where they live in hiding until Beira next comes to drink from the Well of Youth. Old and spent, Beira has no strength left to battle them, so they return to Scotland to rule between Imbolc and Samhain, when the Queen of Winter rises once more.

On the Isle of Mull lies the Carn na Caillich, where Beira apparently dropped stones while building a bridge. And on the Isle of Skye there are two mountains named after her, both known as Beinn na Caillich.

✦ CUSTOMS RELATING ✦
TO THE CAILLEACH

Stories of the Cailleach or Beira are thought to be more than 3,000 years old and there are still echoes of these tales throughout the Scottish landscape and culture.

In Glen Lyon in Perthshire, in a hidden valley called Glen Cailleach, there is a shrine to the powerful Queen of Winter.

The shrine consists of a small hut or shieling with a "family" of small standing stones representing the Cailleach, the Bodach and their children. Locals and folklorists still observe the ritual of shutting the stones carefully inside the hut between Samhain and Beltane to protect them during the winter, bringing them out again to gaze over the valley in the spring and summer months.

This is thought to be one of the oldest Celtic folk practices still observed in Scotland today.

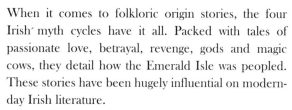

✦ THE ORIGINS OF IRELAND ✦

When it comes to folkloric origin stories, the four Irish´ myth cycles have it all. Packed with tales of passionate love, betrayal, revenge, gods and magic cows, they detail how the Emerald Isle was peopled. These stories have been hugely influential on modern-day Irish literature.

The first of the four myth cycles of Ireland, known as *The Mythological Cycle*, was written down by Christian scholars in the eleventh century and collects much older folk tales about the invasion and settlement of Ireland.

It contains stories and poems about the Tuatha Dé Danann, the supernatural early inhabitants of Ireland. Godlike and skilled in magic, the Tuatha Dé Danann ruled over Ireland peacefully before they were defeated by the Milesians from Iberia, the forebears of the modern-day Irish.

The defeated Tuatha Dé Danann retreated into the Otherworld, another realm that exists in parallel with ours. Here, they could continue to practise magic and live without fear of human interference, only showing themselves to humans if they chose to.

The Tuatha Dé Danann are thought to be the ancestors of the Aos Sí, the fairy folk or "people of the mounds" who live in fairy forts beneath the ground, using fairy mounds to pass between our world and theirs.

As original inhabitants of Ireland, the Aos Sí have a strong bond with the landscape and are fiercely protective of it. Creatures of Irish folklore such as banshees, leprechauns and the far darrig are thought to originate from this tradition.

At particular times of year, like Samhain, Beltane and Midsummer, the Aos Sí are believed to be most visible to humans, coinciding with our modern-day Halloween, May Day and Midsummer festivals.

CHAPTER TWO:

THE NATURAL WORLD

The landscape of the British Isles is amazingly diverse. Travel its length and breadth and you'll find everything from craggy coastline and quiet rolling pasture, to mudflats, moorland, snowy peaks and wooded valleys, all packed in, side by side.

This hugely varied terrain, and the astonishing range of plants and creatures it supports, has deeply shaped the stories shared by the people who have lived there. Everyone from the Celts, Picts, Romans and Vikings, right through to modern-day British storytellers, draw symbolism and story from its crags and coast, meadows and moor.

Take to the islands' lanes and byways and you'll find every barrow has its resident spirit, every hole its boggart and every stream its kelpie or grindylow. Even the place names reflect a passion for folk tales, like Devil's Dyke in Sussex, the Giant's Causeway in Northern Ireland and Mermaid's Pool in the Peak District.

✦ THE GREEN MAN ✦

With his face of leaves and twigs, and creepers sprouting from his mouth, the Green Man is an ancient embodiment of masculinity and nature. He's thought to be the guardian of the rivers and forests in Britain. He also appears as a symbol of fertility and rebirth as winter ends and spring returns.

Beltane or May Day celebrations across the country still often feature a Green Man, either as a costumed figure who takes part in the parade or through images of him woven into the decorations of the event.

The Green Man is a widely recognized symbol in Britain and is usually depicted with a bearded face thick with oak leaves and acorns, both of which are sacred symbols in Celtic society. As well as having healing properties, oak trees were believed to be portals to other realms and were used by Druids, the Celtic religious class, in their rites and ceremonies.

Carvings of the Green Man image are common in medieval churches in the UK. This has led researchers to speculate that the figure represents a bridge between ancient pagan beliefs and the Christianity which replaced them.

There are some good examples of Green Man carvings in St Davids Cathedral in Pembrokeshire, St Pancras Church in Widecombe-in-the-Moor in Devon and Rosslyn Chapel in Midlothian.

It's thought the May King, who sits alongside the May Queen at British May Day celebrations, is just another version of the Green Man.

The Green Man is also sometimes known as the Green Knight or Jack in the Green.

✦ THE GIANTS WHO ✦ SHAPED THE LANDSCAPE

British folk tales are full of giants whose large-scale exploits explain how the landscape came to be the way it is. Spot an unusual hill, boulder or dip, and you can almost guarantee that some irate giant did something or other to cause the feature to form.

THE GIANT'S CAUSEWAY

One of the UK's most famous giant-based folk tales is the origin story of the Giant's Causeway in County Antrim.

According to folklore, the thousands of interlocking hexagonal columns of basalt rock which make up the Giant's Causeway were the handiwork of Irish giant Finn McCool. Back in the mists of time, McCool built the Giant's Causeway so he could cross the Irish Sea to take on his great rival: the Scottish giant Benandonner.

As the legend goes, when McCool got to Scotland he saw that Benandonner was much bigger than he had anticipated. Not fancying the fight after all, he hurried back to Ireland with the enormous Scottish giant in hot pursuit.

Arriving back in Ireland just ahead of his foe, McCool got his wife to hastily disguise him as a baby, bizarrely. She swaddled him and laid him in a giant cot, just as Benandonner arrived.

The deception turned out to be a smart move as the pursuing Benandonner went off the idea of a battle when he saw the huge baby, reasoning that, given the size of the baby, its father must be huge.

So Benandonner turned tail and ran back to Scotland, ripping up the causeway as he went in case McCool followed.

THE WELSH GIANT RHITTA GAWR

Yr Wyddfa, or Mount Snowdon as it's known in English, is rumoured to be the burial mound of Welsh supergiant Rhitta Gawr.

According to legend, Rhitta Gawr was a terrible warmongering giant who ruled over what is called Eryri or Snowdonia National Park. His was a reign of terror against neighbouring kingdoms.

He first attacked warring local kings Nynniaw and Peibaw, destroying their armies and taking their beards as trophies, which he made into a fetching cap for himself. Next, he took on a further 26 kings of Britain and their armies in turn, each of which he defeated with his terrible might.

He took the beard of each of the 26 defeated kings and made them into a thick cloak for himself to keep off the winter cold.

As winter progressed, Rhitta Gawr wanted more beards to patch his cloak.

"Get me more kings!" he roared to his hangers-on. However, the only still-living king that anyone could think of was the legendary King Arthur.

"Come here and give me your beard!" Rhitta Gawr demanded in a message to Arthur.

"Not likely!" King Arthur replied, so offended at the suggestion that he marched to Snowdonia to teach Rhitta Gawr a lesson.

The result was a fearsome duel between giant and king, in which Arthur raised up his sword and struck the giant so hard he was effectively cut in two. According to legend, Arthur then ordered a cairn to be built over the giant's body. This was known as Gwyddfa Rhudda (Rhitta's Cairn).

Over the intervening centuries, the name of Rhudda was forgotten and Gwyddfa Rhudda became known as Yr Wyddfa.

THE GIANTS OF WHEELDALE MOOR

On the heather-covered moors above Whitby in North Yorkshire lies another mysterious causeway. Possibly an old Roman road, this intriguing stone track runs for a mile or so, complete with a paved surface and drainage ditches at the side.

According to folklore, this causeway was the work of local giantess Bell and her husband, Wade. Apparently, Bell and Wade built the road so that Bell could cross the moor to milk her giant cow who lived on its windswept heights. Stray boulders seen in the area are said to be stones that Bell accidentally dropped from her apron as she went along, laying the road.

Wade was credited with building Mulgrave Castle, while Bell apparently built Pickering Castle on the other side of the moor. In the eighteenth century, a whale's jawbone displayed in nearby Mulgrave Castle was reputed to be one of the ribs of Bell's enormous cow.

✦ HILL FIGURES ✦

A series of mysterious, evocative chalk hill figures can be found cut into the landscape across southern England. Usually depicting giants and horses, these mystical pieces of land art are thought to have their roots in pre-Roman times.

THE CERNE GIANT

One of the most famous chalk figures is the Cerne Giant, an enormous 55-metre (180-foot) image of a naked man armed with a club, which is cut into the hillside above Cerne Abbas in Dorset.

Research by the National Trust indicates the figure was probably made in the late Saxon period, and the inclusion of a large erection has led people to believe that it might be a fertility symbol.

In the past, couples visited the site to help them conceive and it's still used today by local morris dancers for their May Day celebrations.

THE UFFINGTON WHITE HORSE

Travel across the Berkshire Downs and you'll catch a glimpse of a dramatic chalk horse leaping across the slopes of a dry valley. Known as the Uffington White Horse, this striking hill figure is as ancient as it is intriguing, and dates back to the Bronze Age.

The Uffington White Horse is part of a series of ancient remains in the area. Nearby Dragon Hill, with its white chalk scar on the top, is said to be where St George slew the dragon. The dragon's blood is supposed to have scorched the grass, preventing it from growing back. The hill is also rumoured to be the burial place of Uther Pendragon, King Arthur's father.

The area is the site of an Iron Age hill fort known as Uffington Castle, as well as a series of ancient burial mounds and a dry valley with steep rippled sides, known as the Giant's Steps.

LONG MAN OF WILMINGTON

The South Downs in Sussex is home to another huge chalk hill figure, known as the Long Man of Wilmington.

He stands 72 metres (235 feet) high. His origins are shrouded in mystery. Some people believe he may be Roman, as a similar image has been found on Roman coins; others believe he is Anglo-Saxon in design, as his likeness has been discovered on pottery of the period.

Another theory is that he was created between the eleventh and fifteenth centuries by monks at the nearby Wilmington Priory.

Unlike the Cerne Giant, the Long Man has no manhood on display. Legend has it that it was erased in Victorian times for reasons of modesty. There is no evidence to support this theory, however!

During the Second World War, the Long Man was painted green to prevent his identification from above by enemy planes.

THE WHITE HORSE OF KILBURN

Covering about 0.6 hectares (1.6 acres) on Sutton Bank in the North York Moors National Park, the enormous White Horse of Kilburn is thought to be the largest and northernmost of Britain's chalk hill figures.

It was cut in 1857 by the village school master and a team of volunteers, and rumour has it that 20 people could fit on the grassy island that makes up its eye.

Although this horse isn't ancient, it is steeped in folklore. There is a local legend about the devil tricking the abbot of Rievaulx Abbey into riding his white mare over the edge of Sutton Bank one stormy night.

The abbot met his end by drowning in the mysterious Gormire Lake which sits just underneath Sutton Bank, and it is said that the ghost of the mare can still be seen on stormy nights.

Gormire Lake possesses its own legend of a sunken village that is believed to lie hidden in its depths.

✦ APPLE LORE ✦

Southern Britain was once covered by great swathes of apple orchards, each spring brimming with blossom and buzzing with bees. Apples were highly prized as they kept well throughout the winter and they could be made into delicious cider for drinking, cooking with and selling.

The importance of apples and apple trees in Britain is reflected in the number of folk tales and customs that have evolved around them.

The ancient apple custom of wassailing happens after Christmas, around Twelfth Night, and involves banging pots and pans in the orchard to ward off evil spirits, placing cider-soaked bread on the trees and pouring cider on their roots. The tradition began in medieval times to encourage a bumper harvest for the coming year.

After each apple harvest, it's also customary to leave one apple on each tree as a gift for the guardian spirit of the orchard.

✦ THE APPLE TREE MAN ✦

The Apple Tree Man is believed to be the spirit of the oldest apple tree in the orchard. Keep him happy and your trees will fruit well. There are numerous stories about this spirit. In some, he frightens away thieves; in others, he rewards hard-working folk.

The following tale comes from a part of Somerset famous for its apples.

There once lived an old farmer. The farmer had two sons. The eldest was hard-working and kind and the youngest was greedy and selfish.

One spring the old farmer died, leaving all this property to his youngest son as was customary in that area. This son inherited everything except a moth-eaten donkey and an old ox covered in sores, which went to the eldest son. The eldest son also received a ruined cottage surrounded by ancient apple trees, but he had to pay rent to his brother to live there.

The younger son, delighted in his new-found power and wealth, poked fun at his elder brother and demanded a high rent for his tumbledown shack. The elder brother didn't grumble, he merely set to work cutting grass, ash, elm, holly and ivy to feed his ox and ass, and gathering healing herbs to treat their ailments.

As spring turned to summer, his animals thrived. He put them out to pasture in the orchard so the apple trees could be fertilized by their droppings. He pruned the old trees as summer turned to autumn, all the time struggling to find money for his food and rent.

As winter approached, he cut mistletoe from the orchard to sell at market. This brought him some pennies but not enough to survive on. He quietly wondered what would become of him.

As the first snows of December began to fall, he was visited by his younger brother. It was the first time the younger brother had been to see him since their father had died.

"I've heard there's gold buried somewhere on this farm," the younger brother declared, "and I mean to find it. Come Christmas Eve, I'll make your old donkey tell me where the treasure is. They say the beasts can talk at midnight. Wake me just before the clock strikes twelve and there might be a sixpence in it for you. Forget, and you're out on your ear."

With that, he left.

Christmas Eve dawned wet and cold. The elder brother shared what little food he had with his ox and ass and warmed the last of his cider over the stove, seasoning it with cinnamon and cloves.

He poured the mulled cider into his mug and carried it outside into the orchard. Braving the wind and rain, he approached the oldest of the apple trees, pulled a crust of bread from his pocket, dunked it in the cider and placed it in the crook of the branches.

Next, as he tipped the last of the cider on the roots of the tree, he quietly sang the following words:

Bud well, bear well
God send you fare well;
Every sprig and every spray
A bushel of apples next New Year Day.

To his great surprise a dry, cracked voice shouted back, "Ah, thankee. That was a drop o'good."

The elder brother looked around him, sure there was no one else in the orchard. He looked back at the old apple tree and watched as the fissures in the bark formed themselves into a gnarled grin, and two beady, pippy eyes looked out from knots in the wood.

"You take a lookee under these gurt roots of ours. There be the treasure," said the Apple Tree Man, waving his twisted branches toward the middle of the orchard.

The elder brother took up his spade and began to dig where he'd been shown. After a few minutes, his spade struck something hard and up came an old box full of bright gold coins.

"'Tis yours and no one else's," said the Apple Tree Man. "Put'n away safe and bide quiet about 'un."

The elder brother carried the box back to his little shack and hid it, then he returned to the orchard to give his heartfelt thanks.

"'Tis a pleasure," said the Apple Tree Man. "Now go and wake your brother. 'Tis nearly midnight."

The elder brother went off to wake his brother. He then returned to his cottage, collected up the box and left to begin a new life.

The younger brother, meanwhile, hurried out of bed, ran through the orchard and into the barn as the church clock struck midnight. He sat and waited expectantly, his teeth chattering.

Sure enough, after a few moments, the donkey turned to the ox and said: "This gurt greedy fool be wanting us to tell where the treasure is."

"Well he won't never get it," the ox replied, "'cause someone's took it already."

✦ MIGHTY OAKS ✦

Broad, majestic and teeming with wildlife, the oak tree occupies a special place in British folklore.

Oaks were believed to be linked to Thor, the Norse god of thunder, as they were often split by lightning during storms. This is probably more to do with their huge size than any mystical associations.

Oak was also a sacred wood to Druids, the priests, healers and academics of Celtic times. The word "Druid" is even thought to come from the Celtic word for oak, signifying the importance of oaks to ancient Britons.

Druids would apparently seek out oak groves to conduct their rituals in, as they believed oak trees enhanced their power. The mistletoe which grows in oak trees was also held in great reverence: it was seen as a sacred plant and the key to connect them with other worlds.

OAK TALES

Oak trees pop up all over British folklore, from tales like The "Faerie Oak of Corriewater" and The "Ballad of Tam Lin" to the traditional practice of carrying an acorn for good luck.

Legend has it that King Charles II hid in an oak tree at Boscobel House in Shropshire to evade capture by Roundhead soldiers during the English Civil War. As a result, 29 May was declared Oak Apple Day in celebration, and children wore crowns of oak leaves to celebrate the tree's role in saving their king.

ROBIN HOOD'S OAK

Bearing witness to a tumultuous period of history that includes Viking invasions, the Norman Conquest, Henry VIII's reign and two world wars, Britain's largest oak is the Major Oak in Sherwood Forest. Believed to be between 800 and 1,100 years old, this enormous tree has many folk associations.

It was reputedly the home of Robin Hood and his merry men, who camped beneath its spreading boughs and hid from the law inside its huge trunk.

WHATEVER THE WEATHER

Oak trees are also believed to help predict the weather:

> *If the oak is out before the ash,*
> *Then we'll surely have a splash.*
> *If the ash is out before the oak,*
> *Then we'll surely have a soak.*

MORE OAKLORE

- **Merlin's Oak:** Carmarthen in Wales was once the site of a mighty oak named after the Arthurian wizard Merlin. It became linked with the town's fortunes as the local rhyme says: "When Merlin's Oak shall tumble down, then shall fall Carmarthen town."

- **Burning oak logs:** Lighting a fire with oak wood was thought to bring good fortune to a home. For this reason, oak was often chosen as the wood for yule logs.

- **Doors to another realm:** In Celtic mythology, oak trees were believed to be portals to the Otherworld. Stand under an oak in a full moon and you might even see the fairies dancing.

OTHER MYSTICAL TREES

- **Elder:** Elders were believed to be inhabited by a female spirit, a fairy queen, a witch or a crone. It was said that if you fell asleep under an elder tree, you might be spirited away by the fairies. According to superstition, elder wood mustn't be burned as doing so might raise the Devil.

- **Holly:** In Europe, holly is linked to the thunder gods Thor and Taranis, and it was common to plant holly to protect houses from lightning. Holly is also said to be good for taming horses, so horsewhip handles were traditionally made from holly.

- **Rowan:** Rowan trees were believed to protect homes and livestock from witches and other evil spirits. They were often planted near barns to keep herds safe.

- **Beech:** Known as Mother of the Woods or Beech Queen, beech trees were believed to have healing properties and offer protection to travellers. Their twigs were often used for water divining.

✦ HERBLORE ✦

Britain's fields, woodlands and hedgerows are packed with plants and flowers whose appearance and names are as engaging as the folk beliefs attached to them.

SAGE

It was an old English folk custom to eat sage every day in May to ensure longevity. For centuries, people brushed their teeth with it. In the sixteenth and seventeenth centuries, drinking tea made of crushed sage leaves was also believed to treat the plague.

CONKERS

Gloriously glossy and fun to collect, conkers have long been associated in folklore with keeping away spiders and moths, and treating sprains and bruises. It's apparently possible to make soap and shampoo out of conkers, too, as the Vikings did.

BLUEBELLS

Bluebells were believed to be magical, with bells that rang so that the fairy folk could dance. Witches, also, supposedly used them to make their potions.

CLOVER

In Britain, clover has long been a symbol of good luck and prosperity. Finding a four-leaf clover is supposed to bring you good fortune and ward off evil. In British folklore, clover is also associated with love: anyone wishing to glimpse their future partner could do so by placing a four-leaf clover under their pillow at night.

DEVIL'S-BIT SCABIOUS

Commonly found in meadows and marshes around Britain, this bluey-lilac wild flower was once used to treat itchy skin conditions such as scabies. Its name comes from a folk belief that one day the devil bit off its roots, causing them to grow short and truncated.

MISTLETOE

Often found on oaks, mistletoe was favoured by Druids for their religious practices and ceremonies. It was thought to be the key to the Otherworld and its evergreen properties symbolized fertility. This might explain the modern practice of kissing under the mistletoe at Christmas.

✦ TELL IT TO THE BEES ✦

The practice of sharing important news with bees – such as births, deaths and marriages – is a British folk tradition with a long history.

The custom is thought to be Celtic in origin. In Celtic culture, bees were believed to possess ancient wisdom and be capable of travelling between one world and the next, bringing back messages from the gods.

Whenever an important family event took place, British beekeepers would head out to their hive or "skep" and tell their bees the news. There was a common superstition in Scotland that it was vital the bees got news of someone's passing to the spirit world before the funeral took place.

It was also common practice after a wedding to give a piece of wedding cake to the bees, and tell them the names of those who'd tied the knot.

People believed that their bees needed to be treated as part of the family and kept them up to date with domestic news so they remained with the hive and stayed happy and healthy. Beekeeping has been an important part of smallholding in Britain since before the Romans and was a prized pursuit, providing beeswax for candles, soap and ointments, and honey for baking and making mead.

Telling the bees if they had a new mistress or master was thought to be a particularly important practice. When Queen Elizabeth II passed away in September 2022, royal beekeeper John Chapple apparently knocked on each of the five royal hives and said to the 20,000 bees living in each one: "The mistress is dead, but don't you go. Your master will be a good master to you."

CHAPTER THREE:

CREATURES AND MONSTERS

Every new wave of settlers in Britain have brought with them their own tales of strange monsters and magical creatures. Tales of the mythical beasts of Pictish and Celtic stories became mixed with those of Roman, Anglo-Saxon and Viking cultures, resulting in a colourful melting pot of fables populated by all sorts of fantastical beings.

Even when pagan worship moved aside for Christianity, the creatures and monsters of folklore didn't disappear: they simply fled to the margins, continuing to fascinate and frighten in literature, poetry, theatre, art and tales whispered around the fire.

Much-loved writers like J. R. R. Tolkien, J. K. Rowling and Cressida Cowell draw brilliantly on this rich well of beasts to fill their story worlds. The success of their books shows the enduring appeal of these imagined beings.

✦ DRAGONS ✦

Dragons appear in folklore the world over and are sometimes referred to as serpents. Their origin remains a mystery, but some experts believe that they were born from an attempt to explain the existence of natural phenomena like rainbows, shooting stars and comets, or that their stories were inspired by the discovery of huge dinosaur bones.

The dragons of British folklore tend to either be fearsome, fire-breathing ones who love gold and treasure, like the dragon in Beowulf and J. R. R. Tolkien's famous Smaug, or venomous, flightless, creeping serpents like the dragon St George defeats. Such stories often depict dragons terrorizing villages or carrying off young women until they're challenged and defeated by a hero.

Dragons were often referred to in these stories as wurms or wyrms, which are variants of an old word for dragon from the Norse word *ormr*, meaning "serpent".

This well-known folk tale comes from the north-east of England and features a serpent-like dragon called the Lambton Worm.

THE LAMBTON WORM

One Sunday morning, a rebellious boy named John Lambton, who was heir to the Lambton Estate in County Durham, decided to skip church to go fishing.

He made his way along the banks of the River Wear to look for a nice sunny spot to fish. As he walked, he passed an old woman who chastised him for not being in church.

"Nothing good will come from this," the old woman warned him.

John fished happily all morning but didn't catch anything. As the church bells tolled to signal the end of the service, he finally landed something – a small, ugly, black worm. The worm was no bigger than John's thumb and wriggled horribly. He tossed it into a well he passed and made his way home.

The years went by and John forgot all about the worm. He gave up his rebellious ways and went overseas to fight in the crusades, leaving the estate in the care of his father.

Over the years, the worm grew, becoming strong, hungry and vengeful. It had turned the well it inhabited poisonous. Livestock and children started to go missing, and there were stories of a dark beast that was long enough to coil itself seven times around a hill.

In a desperate attempt to free local people from the tyranny of the worm, John's father began a daily ritual of offering the worm the milk of nine good cows from a trough in the courtyard of Lambton Castle. Every evening, the creature would slither across the cobbles and drink the milk before slouching back to the well.

From time to time, brave villagers and local knights would attempt to kill the worm, failing each time. The creature appeared to possess a supernatural ability to regenerate. Each time a piece of it was cut off, the chunk simply reattached itself and the creature fought on more strongly than ever.

When John returned from the crusades, he found the estate in ruin: crops had spoiled, livestock numbers had depleted and villagers were afraid to leave their homes. He listened in horror to reports of a vast, black worm in a well wreaking havoc across the countryside. He suddenly remembered the tiny hideous creature he'd cast aside all those years ago.

Overcome with guilt, John vowed to rid his people of their tormentor and he set off for Durham to seek the advice of a wise woman. The wise woman confirmed that the beast was indeed the same worm. She also told him that to defeat it, he must cover his armour in spikes and fight the beast in the River Wear where it often sat, coiled around a rock.

Finally, she told John that once he'd killed the worm, to avoid a curse that would cause his descendants to die unnatural deaths for nine generations, he must then kill the first living thing he saw.

John thanked the wise woman and headed home to prepare his armour. He also arranged with his father that he would sound his hunting horn three times after vanquishing the worm, so his father could make sure one of their hunting dogs was sent out first.

He set off for the River Wear to do battle with the worm and a fierce struggle in the middle of the fast-flowing water ensued. The terrible worm wrapped its scaly coils around John to crush him. Thanks to John's spiked armour, however, the creature was impaled on the spears and was unable to squeeze him.

John took advantage of the creature's inability to move and slashed at it with his sword. As chunks were sliced off the dreadful worm, they were carried away downstream by the swirling waters, preventing the worm from regenerating and ensuring victory for John.

When he was sure the creature was dead, John climbed out of the river and sounded his hunting horn three times.

In his joy at hearing the horn, John's father forgot all about his promise and dashed out to meet his son. John was terrified when his father appeared first instead of his dog and he chose to bring the curse down upon his family rather than harm his father.

It's said that for at least three generations the earls of Durham died unnatural deaths, once by drowning and twice in battle, and all because of the terrible Lambton Worm and the questionable choices made by John Lambton in his youth.

✦ BROWNIES ✦

Brownies, or hobs, appear in Scottish and English folklore and are little household fairies or goblins who live in unused parts of a home and secretly help with domestic tasks. It's said that they are very hard-working, prefer not to be noticed by the humans they serve and generally come out at night.

According to some folk tales, they can be capricious and easily offended, and will leave a house forever if they feel insulted. The house and its residents will then suffer as a result. Attempting to name a brownie or hob, thank it directly or offer it clothing to wear are some of the ways in which it could become upset.

In parts of Britain, it was customary to leave out a dish of milk or cream to keep the house brownie happy.

The house elves in the fictional world created by J. K. Rowling share many characteristics with the brownies of folklore.

✦ BOGGARTS ✦

Boggarts are another small goblin-like house spirit from British folklore. They are also known as boggles, bugbears or bogeys.

Unlike brownies, boggarts have no desire to help the humans that they live with. Their main aim is to make things as difficult as possible by doing things like souring the milk, interfering with livestock, breaking furniture and slamming doors at night.

In some stories, boggarts are simply brownies who have been seriously offended by the family they live with. Sometimes it's possible to turn a boggart back into a brownie through acts of generosity and kindness, but in other cases the only way to deal with a boggart is to hang a horseshoe above the door, leave salt on the doorstep or move house.

According to some folklorists, even moving house won't work with a particularly stubborn boggart as the spirit will simply follow the afflicted family to their new home.

✦ SELKIES ✦

Selkies are thought to originate from Celtic mythology and are beautiful, mysterious shape-shifter who can transform from seal to human by shedding their skin. They're often depicted as alluring women who prove irresistible to human men. Matches between human and selkie rarely go well, however, as the selkie will always dream of returning to the sea.

THE SELKIE BRIDE

One of the best-known selkie stories is that of the Selkie Bride.

As the tale goes, one day a Scottish fisherman heard beautiful singing coming from a hidden cove and saw a group of selkie women basking in the sun. As soon as they spotted him, they disappeared into the sea, but not before the fisherman found and picked up one of their skins.

The young selkie woman whose skin he had, approached him and begged him to return her skin so she might go back into the sea. The fisherman was mesmerized by her loveliness and refused. He confessed his love for her and pleaded with her to become his wife.

The selkie woman finally agreed, so they married and took a cottage together. The fisherman carefully hid her selkie skin from her so that she couldn't return to the sea and they had several children. Their life together might have been a happy one, except for the fact that the selkie woman was often sad and would sit for hours gazing out to sea.

Her youngest child saw his mother's sadness and asked her why she looked at the sea and shed tears. She told her son that she was a selkie and that she longed to return to the sea but couldn't because her skin had been taken from her.

The boy found the skin and returned it to his mother. The selkie woman put it on and returned to the sea, leaving both her children and her husband forever.

SELKIE MEN

In some folk tales, selkies are men who are irresistible to human women. The folklore of Orkney contains stories of selkie men who cast their skins aside to come ashore to seek out unsatisfied human women to lie with.

In order to summon a selkie man, a human woman is supposed to cry seven tears into the ocean. Her selkie lover will then appear. The number seven appears quite often in selkie tales. In some stories, selkies can only turn into their human forms once every seven years; in others, they will only appear to their human lovers during a "seventh stream", which is an unusual pattern of weather that leads to changes in tides.

It is said that Midsummer's Eve and full moons are the best time to see selkies.

✦ KELPIES ✦

Kelpies are shape-shifting water spirits that are common in Scottish folklore. They are also sometimes known as water horses and are believed to live in lochs, rivers and other stretches of water.

Kelpies are capable of living underwater and shape-shifting into a human form at will. They are usually portrayed as being horses and when they assume their human form, they're said to retain their hooves – a tell-tale sign that they are not what they appear to be. When in horse form, they are recognizable by the waterweeds and shells in their mane.

They're thought to be very alluring and attractive to the opposite sex, and keen to appear fun and playful to children. Various stories recount how they use their wiles to lure their human victims into drowning.

It's alleged that the only way to defeat a kelpie is to kill it with an iron weapon or silver bullet, or to capture it with a harness stamped with the cross.

✦ BANSHEES ✦

Banshees are female fairies or wraiths who wail, shriek or "keen", and clap their hands to foretell a death in the family or announce when someone has died. The name banshee comes from the Old Irish *ben síde*, which means "woman of the fairy mound".

A banshee is often described as an old woman in a cloak with long hair, which she combs as she wails. Her face is said to be dreadful to look at, with eyes red from crying. Her wails are described as unbearably sad and she usually appears at night to bring her message.

In Scottish folk tales, she's known as the Bean Nighe, or Washerwoman, and she stands at a ford or stream trying to wash blood from the clothes of the person whose death she foretells.

The Bean Nighe was said to be the spirit of a woman who died in childbirth. Her early death meant that she was condemned to foretell the deaths of others until the time when she would naturally have passed away.

✦ MERMAIDS ✦

Mermaids are one of the best-known figures of folklore. Britain's identity as an island nation means its coastal towns and villages echo with tales of these wild and beautiful half-human women who interact with fishing communities, with a variety of results.

In these stories, mermaids are usually captivating aquatic creatures who have the head and upper body of a human and the tail of a fish. They are often described as having beautiful singing voices and long hair, which they like to comb as they sing.

Unlike sirens, who lure sailors to their deaths, mermaids are sometimes depicted as being kind and helpful to the humans they meet. This next folk tale features one such benevolent type of mermaid.

✦ THE MERMAID ✦
AND THE APPLE TREE

Many tides ago, near Cornaa on the Isle of Man, there lived a fishing family. The father was a skilled fisherman. Every morning he would go out in his boat with a basket of apples, and every evening he'd return with a boatload of fish.

When he got too old to fish, his sons took over the boat and went out into Bulgham Bay. The sons didn't have the skills of their father and gradually their catch dwindled away to nothing. The family went hungry and began to despair.

One day, the youngest son was out in the boat alone when he heard a woman's voice coming from behind him. He whipped around in surprise to see a mermaid holding on to the edge of the stern. He was terrified until he saw her calm smile and heard her beautiful voice asking him gently, "Where is your father? Is he well?"

The young man relaxed and he chatted happily with the mermaid until it was time to head home. The mermaid bade him farewell and promised they'd meet again. When the son got home, he told his father what had happened and the old man was delighted.

"Our luck will change from this day forth," he told his son. "Just don't forget to take a basket of apples when you go out in the boat."

The next time the son went fishing, he put the apples in the boat beside him. The mermaid immediately appeared, took the apples and thanked him with these words:

May the luck of the sea be with you,
but don't forgetful be
when bringing the land eggs to the children of the sea.

For many years the two remained friends, and the family enjoyed great fortune with their fishing. One day, however, the young man decided to leave Cornaa. He wanted to see the world and planned to set sail for distant lands.

The mermaid was distraught to hear the news that she would lose both her cherished companion and her beloved "land eggs".

To soften the blow of parting, the son planted an apple tree for the mermaid overlooking the water where she liked to play. The son gently told her that when the apples ripened, they would fall down into the water and she could gather them up for herself.

He left, and the mermaid waited for the apples to ripen. She was often heard singing sadly beneath the apple tree, lamenting her lost companion while she waited for the "land eggs" to fall.

Spring came and went, and although the tree bore beautiful blossom, it produced no fruit. The same happened the following year, and the mermaid's sorrow grew.

After the second autumn, the mermaid could wait no longer. As the days shortened, she swam out into Bulgham Bay in search of her lost playmate.

Neither the young man nor the mermaid were ever seen again. The apple tree, however, grew good and strong, and the very next year it began to produce fruit. Each September, glossy red apples ripened and dropped down into the water below – land eggs for the children of the sea.

GRINDYLOWS

Mermaids aren't the only water creatures in British folklore. There are also grindylows: strange water spirits who inhabit pools, lakes or marshes.

Lacking the gentle spirit and grace of their sea-dwelling sisters, grindylows lie in wait in their marshy homes to grab unsuspecting children and pull them to their deaths. They're often depicted as being small and human-like with scaly skin, sharp claws and strong arms which they use to hold on to their victims.

Grindylows are most common in the folk tales of Yorkshire and Lancashire. It's been suggested that their name might derive from the monster Grendel in the Old English epic poem, Beowulf.

✦ LEPRECHAUNS ✦

Leprechauns feature primarily in Irish folk tales and are thought to be part of the world of the Aos Sí, or fairy folk, descended from the Tuatha Dé Danann – the supernatural deities who once inhabited Ireland.

Like brownies and banshees, leprechauns are solitary fairies who only show themselves to humans when they choose to. Unlike kelpies or boggarts, they are not usually malevolent, choosing to play tricks on people rather than harming them. They often inhabit rural areas, living in caves, trees or hedgerows where they go about the business of shoemaking.

In modern folklore, they're usually depicted as little men with beards and green clothes, but before the twentieth century they were believed to wear red.

Find a leprechaun and you might be in
with a chance of extracting three wishes
from him. Be careful though, leprechauns
have a reputation for cunning and will go
to any length to avoid being captured.

✦ PIXIES ✦

In British folklore, pixies – sometimes called "piskies" or "pigsies" in parts of the West Country – are small, usually harmless fairies who love to sing and dance.

They are most prevalent in the folk tales of Devon and Cornwall, and they're thought to live in mounds or barrows in the countryside, like the Aos Sí in Ireland.

According to local lore, there were once pixies who lived across Exmoor and Dartmoor and who rode the native wild ponies.

Since June 1954, Pixie Day has been celebrated in the village of Ottery St Mary in east Devon. Legend has it that the village was once occupied by pixies. When the villagers built a church, the pixies believed that every time the church bells rang one of them would die. So on Midsummer in 1454, they kidnapped the bellringers and hid them in a cave, which is still known today as Pixie's Parlour. Fortunately, the bellringers escaped, but the story is still reenacted every year by the villagers.

✦ OGRES ✦

In British folklore, an ogre is a type of unpleasant, brutish and bloodthirsty giant that is always on the lookout for a tasty human to eat. They are often described as being huge, hideous and greedy, and it's thought their name derives from Orcus, the Etruscan god who ate human flesh.

One folk tale from Norfolk tells of how local giant Tom Hickathrift defeated the vicious Ogre of Smeeth using a cartwheel as a shield and an axle as a sword.

According to the story, the Ogre of Smeeth had been tormenting the giant by preventing him from passing with his cart to market across the marshes between King's Lynn and Wisbech. One day, Tom Hickathrift decided that he could no longer live with the tyranny and so in defiance he drove his cart straight across the ogre's land.

On seeing Tom, the ogre was furious. He raced to his lair and seized his club. Tom had no weapons, so he armed himself with parts of his cart and a fierce battle raged between giant and ogre. Despite the ogre's brutality, Tom's size stood him in good stead, and he managed to defeat his evil opponent – slicing off the ogre's head and ridding the area of its oppressor.

The legend of Tom Hickathrift is very real to the residents of Tilney All Saints in Norfolk. It is said that Tom chose the spot where he is supposedly buried by hurling a stone boulder, which lies in the churchyard of the local church in the village. So perhaps there is more truth than myth to the story.

✦ WITCHES ✦

The witches of British folklore fall into two categories: wise and helpful like the woman in the Lambton Worm story, or malicious like the witch who turned a would-be king and his men into the famous Rollright Stones in Oxfordshire – more on that over the page.

As well as being able to perform magic and see into the future, British witches were also believed to be shape-shifters. Across the UK, there are a great number of folk tales about witches who would turn themselves into hares to steal milk, destroy crops or commit other acts of antisocial behaviour.

In these stories, the witch-in-hare-form is often chased by villagers with dogs or shot at with a silver bullet made from a melted-down sixpence or silver button. The witch-hare is usually hurt in the chase but not killed, and always manages to escape into the garden or cottage of an old woman and disappear.

The next day, the old woman is then seen with an injury identical to the one sustained by the hare in the chase. This leads villagers to conclude that she is, in fact, a witch who can shape-shift into a hare at will.

Some folklorists believe that hares became associated with witches because of their uncanny ability to evade capture, their strange habit of standing upright and the way they are sometimes found sitting in a circle as though they are having a meeting or "convocation".

OTHER WITCH BELIEFS

In British folklore, witches are also associated with elder trees. Witches were believed to be able to turn themselves into elder trees at will, and to have the power to conjure up storms by stirring water with an elder twig.

There is a charming belief that witches like to use eggshells, or cockle or mussel shells, as boats. It was once common practice to crush an eggshell after eating an egg to prevent a witch from sailing in it.

✦ THE ROLLRIGHT STONES ✦

There's a mysterious collection of standing stones, called the Rollright Stones, in the Cotswolds. According to legend, an Iron Age king was marching his army over Rollright Hill when a witch barred his path, crying: "Seven long strides shalt thou take and if Long Compton thou canst see, king of England thou shalt be."

On the king's seventh stride, however, a mound rose up, obscuring his view. The witch then turned the king and his troops to stone.

The king became the King Stone, his troops became the King's Men and his knights became the Whispering Knights. The witch turned herself into an elder tree, which still stands in a nearby hedgerow.

According to local lore, it's impossible to count the stones that make up the King's Men. A baker once tried by placing a loaf on each stone. Each time he attempted to collect the loaves, however, he found some had been stolen away by fairies or other spirits.

✦ DEVILISH DOGS ✦

British folklore is full of tales of solitary, red-eyed hellhounds who roam remote spots at night, terrorizing unwary travellers.

One of the most famous of these creatures is East Anglia's Black Shuck, who was first sighted in 1577 in Bungay in Suffolk. According to the legend, the villagers were taking refuge in the church of St Mary from a storm when Black Shuck attacked. Racing down the aisle of the church, he broke the necks of two people at prayer, before setting upon a third man who he left "drawen together and shrunk up, as it were a peece of lether scorched in a hot fire."

Other parts of the country have their own hellish canines. North Yorkshire has the Bargest or Barghest, a huge black dog with large teeth, which is said to be an omen of death and to frequent the medieval snickelways and lanes of York. West Yorkshire, meanwhile, has a similar creature known as Padfoot, who is supposed to linger in front of a house where a death is imminent.

✦ CHURCH GRIMS ✦

In British and Scandinavian folklore, Church Grims are spirits who protect churches and churchyards from the devil and other evildoers.

They are most often seen in their animal form as large black dogs with burning red eyes.

In the sixteenth and seventeenth centuries, it was customary for a real black dog to be buried alive under any new church or churchyard in order to create a Church Grim spirit to protect it from evil.

Excavations of medieval cemeteries have sometimes revealed the skeletons of large dogs, in keeping with this folk belief.

An unusually large dog skeleton was discovered in the graveyard of Leiston Abbey in Suffolk in 2013. It was initially thought to be the remains of Black Shuck, but it is possibly just the remains of a Church Grim.

✦ THE LEGEND ✦
OF KILGRAM BRIDGE

There is a folk tale from North Yorkshire about a large black dog appeasing the devil so that people might cross the River Ure. In the story, the dog is called Grim.

Many attempts had been made to build a strong bridge that would withstand flooding over the River Ure near Jervaulx Abbey, but every attempt had failed. One day the devil offered to build a bridge for the people on the condition that the first living thing to cross it would be sacrificed to him.

The villagers agreed, and when the bridge was finished, they thought long and hard about who should be sacrificed to the devil as payment.

A local shepherd, who had a dog called Grim, swam across the river, knowing that his dog would follow him. Grim duly ran across the bridge in pursuit of his master and was taken up as a sacrifice by the devil.

The bridge was known as Kilgrim Bridge before it was renamed Kilgram Bridge.

✦ THE WILD HUNT ✦

Around Dartmoor and in other rural parts of Britain, it's common to hear tales of the Wild Hunt. This is a terrifying horseback hunt that tears across the countryside at night, led by a spectral leader and followed by wraith-like riders with baying hounds known as the Gabriel Hounds or Wisht Hounds.

The appearance of the Wild Hunt is thought to portend disaster, signalling the coming of war or death. The leader of the hunt varies from story to story: sometimes it is Herne the Hunter and at other times it's the devil or even King Arthur, acting under a curse.

Herne the Hunter is a well-known figure in the south of England. He's characterized by the antlers he wears on his head and his ability to lead the Gabriel Hounds and other spirits. In some stories he was once the king's favourite keeper in Windsor Great Park but his great skill with the deer made the other keepers jealous. One day they paid a wizard to destroy Herne's gifts, causing Herne to hang himself in despair from an oak tree in the park.

Since he met his unhappy end, Herne is said to rage across the countryside with the souls of the jealous keepers as his riders. The Gabriel Hounds are said to be the spirits of unbaptized babies and other unquiet beings.

Prior to the outbreaks of the First and Second World Wars, sightings of the Wild Hunt were reported a number of times across the county of Berkshire. Some folklorists believe that Midsummer and Samhain – or Halloween – are the best times of year to see the hunt.

✦ WILL-O'-THE-WISP ✦

In British folklore, a Will-o'-the-Wisp is a strange, ethereal light which appears at night and hovers over marshes, low-lying areas and woodland to lead travellers astray.

The light of the Will-o'-the-Wisp resembles a lantern or lamp light. Following it will likely lead you to your doom by luring you over a cliff or into fast-flowing water. Some people believed that Will-o'-the-Wisps were the unquiet spirits of those who'd died but hadn't made it into either heaven or hell. Instead, these spirits were said to rove the earth after dark, preying on the unwary.

Regional variations of the name Will-o'-the-Wisp include The Hobby Lantern, Hinkypunk, Jack-o'-Lantern and Jenny with the Lantern.

Similar lights seen in churchyards are known in folklore as corpse lights. They were thought to foretell an imminent death and mark the path of a coming funeral.

✦ THE LOCH NESS MONSTER ✦

The Loch Ness Monster, or Nessie as it's known, is possibly the most famous monster in modern-day Scottish folklore. Catapulted to fame by a sighting reported in *The Inverness Courier* in 1933, a whole cult of folklore has grown up around it.

Nessie is believed to be a large sea monster or serpent which lives in the depths of Loch Ness. Believers claim it was first mentioned in an account of St Columba's life written in the seventh century. This chronicle states that a man was out swimming in the River Ness one day when he was attacked by a water beast. St Columba then made the sign of the cross and the beast halted and disappeared.

More recent sightings of the Loch Ness Monster include those captured on video, camera and by sonar, all of which remain unconfirmed. There are numerous theories about what Nessie might be, including a giant squid, a plesiosaur and an eel.

Folklorists claim that stories about kelpies living in Loch Ness have existed for centuries, and that these have likely fed into the Nessie myth.

CHAPTER FOUR:

LEGENDARY HEROES

Folklore and folk tales are an age-old way of exploring both the world around us and the power within us. Creating heroes and villains to embody human values, characteristics and emotions is a way for us to play out our fears and fantasies, allowing us to live dangerously from the safety of our own firesides.

It's no surprise then that British folklore contains a heady roster of legendary heroes and heroines who symbolize the best and worst of our human desires. From mighty wizards like Merlin and Morgan le Fay, and gutsy warriors like King Arthur and Boudicca, to unlikely everyday heroes like Dick Whittington.

By following these archetypal characters through their challenges and quests to the ultimate fulfilment of their destiny, maybe we can learn something valuable about ourselves and the landscape of Britain.

✦ KING ARTHUR ✦

King Arthur remains one of the best-known figures of British folklore. Famed for his prowess in battle, desire for truth and justice, and his extraordinary sword Excalibur, Arthur first appears in a ninth-century history of Britain written by a Welsh monk called Nennius.

This formidable warrior then reappears in the tenth-century Welsh chronicles and in Geoffrey of Monmouth's *History of the Kings of Britain*. According to Geoffrey, Arthur was conceived in Tintagel Castle in Cornwall with the help of the wizard Merlin and became a great leader who led the Britons against the Anglo-Saxons in the fifth and sixth centuries.

Geoffrey of Monmouth also describes how Arthur enjoyed a great and glorious reign as a warrior king before being betrayed and defeated in a final battle by his own son, Mordred. Upon his death, Arthur was taken to the Isle of Avalon by the healer and sorceress, Morgan le Fay.

After the twelfth century, King Arthur myths continue to be told and retold, populated by characters such as the wizard Merlin, Arthur's wife Guinevere, Launcelot and the Knights of the Round Table, all played out in the mythical court of Camelot.

Some of the best-known King Arthur tales include the story of how he was able to pull a mysterious sword from a stone as a young boy, when everyone else had failed. This uncanny ability revealed him to be the true king of the Britons, and heir to Uther Pendragon's throne.

Another famous Arthurian legend is that of "Sir Gawain and the Green Knight", which comes from a thirteenth-century English poem. In this story, Arthur is challenged to a fight to the death by a strange green knight who appears during a New Year's feast. Sir Gawain steps in to take up the challenge for Arthur, however, and undertakes a strange journey of self-discovery.

It is often said that King Arthur is sleeping and will one day return to rule again. His suggested locations include Cadbury Castle in Somerset, a cave near Alderley Edge in Cheshire and under Richmond Castle in Yorkshire.

✦ MERLIN ✦

Merlin is a powerful wizard and prophet from the King Arthur stories. He first appears in a manuscript by Geoffrey of Monmouth called *Prophetiae Merlini* in which he is said to possess supernatural powers because, even though his mother was human, his father was an incubus demon.

Geoffrey's later work, *History of the Kings of Britain*, goes on to tell us that Merlin was born in Carmarthen and created the mighty Stonehenge by conjuring its giant stones from Ireland to mark the burial place of Aurelius Ambrosius.

Later legends written down by Thomas Malory recount how Merlin became chief advisor to the young King Arthur, revealing prophesies to him, including that of his own death at the hands of his son, Mordred.

Merlin is thought to have inspired both
J. R. R. Tolkien's wizard Gandalf and
J. K. Rowling's Albus Dumbledore.

✦ MORGAN LE FAY ✦

Enchantress, temptress and shape-shifter, Morgan le Fay, is a fascinating female character from the world of Arthurian folklore. Morgan, also known as Morgana, first appeared in Geoffrey of Monmouth's *Vita Merlini* where she was described as a magical healer who lived with her eight sisters on the Isle of Avalon.

Other later Arthurian legends cast Morgan as Arthur's supernatural half-sister, born from his mother Igraine's first marriage to Gorlois. She is usually said to possess the ability to perform magic, fly and shape-shift.

In some folk tales, Morgan comes to Arthur's aid, using her powers for good. In others, she is his enemy, using her magic to thwart Arthur and seize power and glory for herself. Most versions of the story agree, however, that when Arthur is finally killed by his own son, Mordred, it is Morgan who takes him back to Avalon to be healed.

Some folklorists believe that Morgan is based on the Celtic-Irish warrior goddess Morrígan.

✦ MABON ✦

Mabon ap Modron is a hero from the Welsh folk tale cycle, *The Mabinogion*. He is described as a young warrior and son of Modron, who he was stolen from when he was only three nights old, to be kept prisoner in the Otherworld.

The story of "Culhwch ac Olwen" tells of how Mabon was rescued by King Arthur and his knights as part of a series of impossible tasks given to them by the giant Ysbaddaden. The knights question the wisest animals on earth to discover Mabon's whereabouts and are eventually led to his prison by the salmon of Llyn Llyw.

Once freed, Mabon plays a vital role in capturing the mythical wild boar Twrch Trwyth, who has a comb, scissors and a razor between his ears in the final task set by Ysbaddaden.

The autumn equinox, which falls on 21 September in the northern hemisphere, is sometimes called Mabon. Some folklorists believe it was at this time of year that Mabon was rescued from prison.

✦ ROBIN HOOD ✦

Robin Hood has captured popular imagination since he first entered British folklore in the fourteenth-century poem by William Langland, "Piers Plowman". Since the outlaw's early appearance in medieval poems and ballads, he's gone on to become the swashbuckling hero of countless films, books, songs and TV series.

Robin Hood, or Robin of Locksley as he's sometimes known, is portrayed as a dashing figure dressed in a feathered cap and a coat of Lincoln green. He is described as an outstanding archer and swordfighter, and champion of the poor. Robin Hood stories usually involve him defending the vulnerable, rescuing captives and avoiding arrest by the cruel and corrupt Sheriff of Nottingham and evil King John.

Many Robin Hood tales also include a band of merry men who supposedly lived with him in the greenwood. His main followers include Little John, Will Scarlet, Friar Tuck and Alan-a-Dale. Later stories also include a love interest for Robin in the form of the bright and feisty Maid Marian.

Interestingly, Maid Marian was originally a British folk character in her own right who, before her association with Robin Hood, featured in medieval May Day celebrations.

According to many versions of the Robin Hood myth, Sherwood Forest in Nottinghamshire was the home of the outlaw and his merry men. They would hide out from the law in the forest's 100,000 acres, using their skill as rangers to survive and evade capture. The ancient and magnificent Major Oak in Sherwood Forest is thought to have been one of their hiding places.

Other sources claim Robin Hood actually came from Yorkshire, with mentions of Barnsdale and Doncaster appearing in some of the early ballads. The existence of both Robin Hood's Well and Robin Hood's Bay in Yorkshire also points to a strong connection with the area.

✦ TOM THUMB ✦

Tom Thumb is an old character from British folklore who later made his way into fairy tales and nursery rhymes.

Most stories about Tom Thumb begin by telling us that he was a boy no bigger than his father's thumb, who possessed extraordinary brains and skill. Sometimes these powers are attributed to Merlin, who granted Tom's father his heart's desire. Tom's father allegedly told Merlin that all he desired was a son, even if he was no bigger than his thumb.

The sixteenth-century church of Tattershall in Lincolnshire is said to be Tom Thumb's final resting place. Inside the church is the tiny grave of a Tom Thumb who died in 1620, aged 101. Some people believe this is the minute hero's tomb. Others argue that it isn't possible, as Tom Thumb stories predate the seventeenth century.

✦ GUY OF WARWICK ✦

According to folklore, Guy of Warwick was a tenth-century English knight who travelled the world undertaking quests to prove his worth to his lady, Felice. He was popularized in romances from the thirteenth to the seventeenth centuries, and his adventures included slaying dragons and seeing off the savage Dun Cow.

Having proved himself worthy of Felice, Guy returned to England where he and Felice married. After a few years of wedded bliss, Guy began to feel remorse for his violent past and, to make amends, he decided to undertake a pilgrimage to the Holy Land.

Guy was absent for many years and returned to England just in time to help King Athelstan rout a horde of Viking invaders at Winchester. After this, Guy became a hermit, living out his days in a cave at Guy's Cliffe on the banks of the River Avon.

Several artefacts said to have belonged to Guy of Warwick are on display at Warwick Castle, including a sword, a fork and a giant porridge pot.

✦ HEREWARD THE WAKE ✦

Sometimes known as Hereward the Outlaw or Hereward the Exile, Hereward the Wake was an Anglo-Saxon noble, who in the eleventh century, led opposition forces against Norman invaders.

Many details of Hereward's early life have been lost, but manuscripts such as the *Gesta Herewardi*, written in the twelfth century, tell us that Hereward was born in Lincolnshire of noble birth and that he was sent into exile for wayward behaviour around the age of eighteen.

During his exile, Hereward travelled through Cornwall, Ireland and Flanders having many adventures along the way, including fighting a huge bear and saving a Cornish princess from a loveless marriage.

Hereward then became a mercenary for Baldwin V of Flanders, fighting campaigns and undertaking expeditions in his name. When Baldwin V died, Hereward returned to England, only to discover that his family had been murdered and his lands had been taken by the Normans.

According to legend, Hereward then took up arms and killed 15 Norman soldiers as they drank and boasted of their victory. After this, Hereward raised a small army and was knighted by his uncle in Peterborough Abbey.

The *Gesta Herewardi* then tells of how Hereward, now a rebel leader, was pursued by the Norman lord William de Warenne and his brother-in-law Frederick. According to the text, Hereward tricked and killed Frederick and escaped from William by unhorsing him with a single arrow shot.

So Hereward then called upon the Danish king Sweyn II to provide an army to help him establish a stronghold on the Isle of Ely. The Danish king obliged, and the Danish forces and Hereward attacked and sacked Peterborough Abbey, which was then in the hands of the Normans.

Another Saxon leader, Morcar, Earl of Northumbria, joined forces with Hereward and together they mounted a defence of the Isle of Ely against the Norman king, William the Conqueror.

The rebel forces were able to hold out against the Normans thanks to their excellent position on high ground surrounded by water-logged marshes. According to local lore, the Normans tried to construct wooden walkways over the fens, yet these simply sank, so they had to resort to using witches to curse the rebels – but this didn't work either.

Hereward and Morcar were ultimately betrayed, however, by a local abbot who, in exchange for lands, provided the Normans with knowledge of a secret route through the boggy fens.

Morcar was arrested, but Hereward escaped. As the story goes, he then roamed the fens for many years living as an outlaw figure and evading capture.

Interest in Hereward the Wake was revived in Victorian times with the publication of the novel *Hereward the Wake: Last of the English* by Charles Kingsley. This romantic, swashbuckling epic paints Hereward as the archetypal British underdog hero: brave, just and a defender of the helpless.

✦ HAVELOK THE DANE ✦

Havelok the Dane is a Lincolnshire folk hero who was made famous in a thirteenth-century English poem "The Lay of Havelok the Dane".

According to the story, Havelok was the son of the just and noble King Birkbein of Denmark. Birkbein died when Havelok was just three years old, leaving Havelok and his two sisters in the care of Godard, a wealthy noble, who was appointed ruler of Denmark until Havelok came of age.

Godard was cruel and ambitious, however, and decided to betray Havelok and his two sisters. He murdered the two girls in cold blood and then handed the young Havelok to a fisherman named Grim to be drowned at sea.

Grim took the boy but began to doubt his orders when he noticed a cross-shaped birthmark, or "kynemark", on Havelok's shoulder. He also saw that a bright light came from Havelok's mouth when he slept. Grim pondered: "Perhaps this boy is the true king of Denmark?"

Grim decided to save the boy's life and he sailed with Havelok and his own family to England. He landed in Lincolnshire, where he founded the town of Grimsby.

Grim raised Havelok as his own son and he grew into a young man of great height, gentleness and good cheer. His strength and good looks attracted the attention of many nobles.

Meanwhile, the English succession was in disarray. Good King Athelwold had died without an heir and left his throne and his young daughter, Goldborow, in the care of Godrich, Earl of Cornwall. Before his death, Athelwold made Godrich promise that Goldborow would marry no one but the "highest" man in England.

As soon as Athelwold was safely buried, however, Godrich went back on this word and imprisoned Goldborow in a fortress in Dover so he could rule England in her stead.

One day, his royal duties took him to Lincolnshire. There he saw the huge Havelok perform amazing feats of strength in a local stone-throwing contest.

Godrich believed the enormous Havelok was a peasant and cunningly decided to marry Goldborow off to him, believing he could deprive Goldborow of the throne and fulfil his promise to marry her to the "highest" man in England in one fell swoop.

Havelok thought himself too poor to marry but was left with no choice when Godrich threatened him and his family. So Havelok and Goldborow were wed and went to live with Grim's family in Grimsby.

As they lay in bed together, Goldborow saw the strange glow coming from the sleeping Havelok's mouth and noticed the "kynemark" on his shoulder. An angel then told her of Havelok's true identity and destiny as rightful king of Denmark and England. At the same time, Havelok had a dream where he held the kingdom of Denmark in his arms and laid it at Goldborow's feet.

In the morning, the couple told each other of what they'd seen and agreed to set sail for Denmark to recover the crown with the help of Grim's three eldest sons.

When they arrived in Denmark, they were able to prove Havelok's real identity by showing the light that came out of this mouth and his "kynemark" to the Danish nobles. Convinced that Havelok was indeed

Denmark's rightful ruler, the nobles helped him raise an army and together they overthrew Godard the usurper to take back the crown.

The victorious Danish king next turned his attention to the English throne. With his new army he invaded England, aiming to oust Godrich and claim the English crown back for his wife, Goldborow.

Once Godrich had been defeated, Havelok ruled Denmark and England wisely and justly for over 60 years. The couple enjoyed a long and happy marriage.

✦ LADY GODIVA ✦

Lady Godiva was a real-life Anglo-Saxon gentlewoman who lived with her husband, Leofric, Earl of Mercia, in Coventry in the early eleventh century. At the time, she was best known for her philanthropy; she and her husband gave generous donations to various abbeys and monasteries, including Leominster and Chester.

Today, Lady Godiva is better remembered as a figure of folklore who, according to legend, once rode naked through the streets of Coventry in protest against an unfair tax levied by her husband.

The citizens of Coventry were ordered to close their windows and doors so as not to see her pass by. All the townsfolk complied, or so the story goes, except for Tom the Tailor.

Unable to contain his curiosity, Tom the Tailor, it is alleged, peeped out of his window to catch a glimpse of Lady Godiva riding by. This indiscretion is thought to be the origin of the phrase "peeping Tom".

✦ SPRING-HEELED JACK ✦

Spring-heeled Jack is a legend of London folklore who first took hold of the popular imagination in the 1830s. He was said to be a terrible demon-like figure dressed like a gentleman in a long black cloak, with clawed hands and red eyes, who could make incredible leaps over buildings.

Sightings of Spring-heeled Jack were common in London in the 1830s and 1840s, where he was thought to prey on unwary travellers making their way home at night. A cult of fear grew around him and he began to appear as a villain in penny dreadfuls (cheap fantastical literature of the time) and plays performed around the capital.

By the early twentieth century, however, he was increasingly being portrayed as a caped crusader, performing heroic deeds and delivering the innocent from evil. He continues to be thought of in this way, appearing as a hero in modern retellings of his story, such as Philip Pullman's 1989 graphic novel *Spring-Heeled Jack*.

✦ BOUDICCA ✦

An important predecessor of feisty female folklore characters such as Maid Marian and Lady Godiva is the mighty warrior queen Boudicca who led an uprising against the Romans in 60 or 61 AD. Boudicca was probably an honorific title, meaning "victorious woman", rather than her actual name. She was the wife of Prasutagus, king of the Celtic tribe the Iceni, who enjoyed the status of an independent people recognized by Rome. The couple lived in modern-day Norfolk.

When Prasutagus died, the Romans refused to honour his will, which stated that his kingdom should be left jointly to Rome and his two daughters. To subjugate the Iceni, the Romans seized his lands and employed the dual tactics of heavy taxation and general brutality.

Appalled by this, Boudicca raised an army against the Romans and sacked and burned the settlements of Camulodunum (modern-day Colchester), Londinium (London) and Verulamium (a Roman town south of St Albans).

Although Boudicca's army enjoyed early victories and were likely to have been the bigger force at first, they were eventually defeated by Roman battalions deployed by Governor Suetonius. The Romans were merciless in victory, killing every woman, child and animal linked to the rebellion. Boudicca died either by poison or from an illness not long afterward.

Since stories of her uprising first appeared in the histories of Roman writers, Tacitus and Cassius Dio, Boudicca has gone on to become an important cultural symbol in British folklore, representing freedom from oppression. Her image as a warrior queen and defender of the helpless was taken up by the suffragettes in the early twentieth century as they campaigned to secure the vote for women in Britain. A famous statue of Boudicca riding into battle in a horse-drawn chariot stands on Westminster Bridge in London.

✦ BEOWULF ✦

The legend of the brave warrior who frees his people from the tyranny of an all-powerful monster is a common theme in folk tales. The story of the hero Beowulf, who defeats the dreadful beast Grendel and his mother, is probably one of the best-known examples of this in English. This tale has gone on to inspire re-tellings by figures like William Morris, Seamus Heaney and J. R. R. Tolkien.

The tale of Beowulf is first recorded in an epic poem written in Old English by an unknown author sometime between the eighth and eleventh centuries. The story is set in Scandinavia in the sixth century and tells of how Beowulf, hero and warrior of the Geat tribe, frees the Danes from the terrible monster Grendel, who has been attacking King Hrothgar's mead hall and murdering his people.

Beowulf goes on to defeat Grendel's mother, another terrible creature, who comes to seek revenge for her son's death. He then returns victorious to Geatland to be crowned king of his own people. Here, he rules wisely and justly until a terrible fire-breathing, poisonous dragon attacks his people and he is killed after vanquishing it in a final, terrible battle.

Beowulf has all the typical characteristics of an Anglo-Saxon hero; he is physically strong, incredibly brave, determined, wise and selfless.

He remains a fascinating figure in British folklore, inspiring many works of literature and film, including the 2007 movie *Beowulf*, written by Neil Gaiman and Roger Avary, and the 2018 feminist retellings of the Beowulf story, *The Mere Wife* by Maria Dahvana Headley.

✦ GRÁINNE O'MALLEY ✦

Pirate queen and fearsome clan chief Gráinne O'Malley, also known as Gráinne Mhaol in Ireland, is a legendary figure in Irish folklore. She is famous for her daring exploits at sea, feminist principles and for defending her territories in Ireland against invaders.

Gráinne was a real person, born in 1530 to a seafaring, landowning family in County Mayo in Ireland. Legend has it that from a young age, she was determined to live a life of adventure: while still a young girl, she petitioned her father to let her join a sea voyage. When he told her that she couldn't because her long hair would get in the way, Gráinne cut her hair off, earning her the nickname Gráinne Mhaol, or "Bald Grace", which stuck.

Other stories tell of Gráinne seeing off Algerian pirates just hours after giving birth on board a ship, defying Gaelic laws by living free of a man's control and sailing to meet Queen Elizabeth I to defend her territories against English annexation.

✦ WILLIAM WALLACE ✦

Immortalized in the 1995 Mel Gibson film *Braveheart*, William Wallace was a Scottish military leader who, in the late thirteenth century, led successful campaigns against the English king Edward I.

Very little is known about who William Wallace really was, but it is certain that in 1297 he led an army against Edward I at the Battle of Stirling Bridge and again in 1298 at the Battle of Falkirk. The Scots scored a resounding victory over the English at Stirling Bridge but were not so fortunate at Falkirk. Wallace was later arrested by Edward I and put to death.

William Wallace's reputation for incredible bravery, skill with a sword and determination to defend his people from oppression has led to him becoming an iconic figure in Scottish folklore.

He is commemorated with the National Wallace Monument near Stirling and immortalized in various works of literature such as a fifteenth-century poem by Blind Harry, the 1793 poem "Scots Wha Hae" by Robert Burns and Sir Walter Scott's 1828 tale "The Story of Sir William Wallace".

✦ DICK WHITTINGTON ✦

The Dick Whittington of English folklore is most often depicted with the cat who helped him make his fortune. Folk tales about Dick Whittington are loosely based on the life of Richard Whittington who lived 1354-1423 and became Mayor of London.

According to legend, Dick Whittington was born a pauper in fourteenth-century England and came to London to seek his fortune, believing the pavements of the capital were "paved with gold". When he arrived, however, he found that life was very hard for a poor lad with no friends or connections.

After wandering the streets, feeling lost and bewildered, Dick finally fell asleep outside the house of Mr Fitzwarren, a wealthy London merchant. The next day, upon finding the lad, Mr Fitzwarren engaged him as a scullion or kitchen boy, and gave him lodgings in his attic.

Work in Mr Fitzwarren's kitchen was hard, and Dick was beaten and harassed by the cook. Nights were no better as his attic room was infested with rats and mice who ran amok and prevented him from sleeping.

Desperate to rid himself of his vermin problem, Dick bought himself a cat with a penny he'd earned shining shoes. It proved a shrewd move, as the cat quickly caught all the rats and mice, and Dick could sleep again.

One day, Mr Fitzwarren told his servants that a ship of his was making a voyage to the Barbary Coast, and he offered them all the chance to buy a stake in the venture. Dick had nothing to offer except his cat, which Mr Fitzwarren accepted, and the cat set sail with the ship.

Back in Mr Fitzwarren's house, things went from bad to worse. The beatings from the cook intensified and one day Dick decided he'd had enough. He gathered up his meagre possessions, intending to walk back home.

The boy set off out of London toward the north, but soon found the uphill route out of the capital exhausting.

He'd got as far as Holloway, when he decided to stop and rest at the foot of Highgate Hill. As he sat and caught his breath, he heard Bow bells chime the hour and it seemed to him the bells called out: "Turn again Whittington, thrice Lord Mayor of London."

Intrigued by the strange message, Dick turned around and made his way back to Mr Fitzwarren's house. When he arrived, he learned that the ship had docked at its destination on the Barbary Coast and that the king there had paid huge sums for the cargo.

The king had also been delighted with Dick's cat, who'd got rid of all the palace's rats and mice. As the story goes, in his joy at being pest-free, the king then paid ten times more again for the cat.

Mr Fitzwarren told Dick that he was now wealthy in his own right, and he recognized him as an equal, allowing him to marry his daughter Alice. Dick went on to become a successful partner in Mr Fitzwarren's business, and, finally, three times Mayor of London, just as the bells had foretold.

There is a stone at the foot of Highgate Hill known as the Whittington Stone, which commemorates the spot where Dick supposedly rested and heard the bells. It bears the legend, "Turn again Whittington, thrice Lord Mayor of London". A statue of Dick Whittington's famous cat was added in 1964.

Dick Whittington remains a popular figure of folklore in London, as his real-life counterpart Richard Whittington significantly improved the lives of the poor in his lifetime by creating a maternity hospital and improving drains and sewers.

✦ FAREWELL ✦

We hope you've enjoyed dipping your toes into the choppy waters of British folklore while keeping one eye out for a kelpie and the other out for Nessie.

From stories about Black Shuck to tales of Beira, the Queen of Winter, these British folk tales are deeply rooted in a half-imagined past when wishes still worked, dragons filled the skies and we had a better understanding of our land.

But what is the future of folklore now that we are less likely to tell stories around the fire and our connection with nature has become evermore distant?

A bright one, hopefully. Folklore is tightly tied to our experience of being human and helps us make sense of our humanity. We're born, we love, we die, and in between we wrestle with all sorts of emotions. Until this changes, we will always need stories to help us understand ourselves and each other.

And while the way we tell stories might have changed, folklore is still most definitely alive and kicking, with re-tellings of ancient tales emerging as graphic novels, TV series and video games, all to rapturous applause year on year. Let's not forget folk customs either. Morris dancing has seen a recent revival and there's a renewed passion for wassailing.

So why not grab a pan and some sticks and go outside? You never know what you might learn about yourself and the world around you.

✦ FURTHER READING ✦

Carolyne Larrington, *The Land of the Green Man: A Journey through the Supernatural Landscapes of the British Isles* (2019, Bloomsbury Academic)

Jacqueline Simpson and Jennifer Westwood, *The Lore of the Land: A Guide to England's Legends, from Spring-heeled Jack to the Witches of Warboys* (2005, Penguin)

Lisa Schneidau, *Botanical Folk Tales of Britain and Ireland* (2018, The History Press)

Neil Philip, *The Watkins Book of English Folktales* (2022, Watkins Publishing)

Neil Philip (ed.), *The Penguin Book of Scottish Folktales* (1995, Penguin)

Pete Castle, *Derbyshire Folk Tales* (2010, The History Press)

Ruth Tongue, *Forgotten Folk-tales of the English Counties* (2020, Routledge)

Sarah Robinson, *The Kitchen Witch: Food, Folklore & Fairy Tale* (2022, Womancraft Publishing)

PODCASTS AND WEBSITES

English Heritage: www.english-heritage.org.uk

The Folklore Podcast: www.thefolklorepodcast.com

The Folklore Scotland Podcast:
www.folklorescotland.com/podcast

The Folklore Society: www.folklore-society.com

Folklore Thursday: www.folklorethursday.com

Loremen: www.loremenpodcast.com

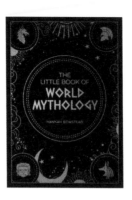

THE LITTLE BOOK
OF WORLD MYTHOLOGY
Hannah Bowstead

ISBN: 978-1-80007-176-6

This handy guide offers readers an accessible introduction to the major world mythologies, their origins, foundational stories and key mythological figures. If you're looking to enrich and expand on your understanding of world history, religion and culture, then this book is an ideal starting point to fill your mind with stories of wisdom and wonder.

THE LITTLE BOOK
OF FAERIES
Francis Nightingale

ISBN: 978-1-83799-377-2

People have long been mesmerized by the magic and mystery of Fae folk. Step into this enchanting world of faeries, pixies, sprites and more with this beginner's guide to the essential history and mythology. Just like the creatures themselves, this book is pocket-sized and full of magic, mirth and mischief.

Have you enjoyed this book?
If so, find us on Facebook at **Summersdale**
Publishers, on Twitter/X at **@Summersdale** and
on Instagram and TikTok at **@summersdalebooks**
and get in touch. We'd love to hear from you!

www.summersdale.com

IMAGE CREDITS